Momentum: The Key to Victory

Momentum: The Key to Victory

John Eckhardt

Crusaders Publications
Chicago, Illinois

Momentum: The Key to Victory
ISBN 0-9630567-8-6
Copyright © 1993 by
John Eckhardt
P.O. Box 7211
Chicago, IL 60680

Published by
Crusaders Publications
P.O. Box 7211
Chicago, IL 60680
U.S.A.

Cover design and book production by
DB & Associates Design Group, Inc.
P.O. Box 52756
Tulsa, OK 74152

Editorial Consultant: Debra Thompson

Contents

Chapter 1
Momentum Brings Impact

The greater the *momentum* of a thing, the greater the *impact* it will have once it reaches its destination. If the Lord's people are to have an IMPACT upon our cities and nation, we must be a people who understand and operate in MOMENTUM. An "impact" is a forceful contact or collision. There will always be a collision between the kingdom of God and the kingdom of darkness.

One of the best examples I can give concerning impact and momentum is that of a hurricane. A hurricane starts as a small storm hundreds of miles offshore in the ocean. As the storm approaches land, it picks up *momentum*. By the time it reaches land it has enough momentum to destroy everything in its path. The *impact* the storm has is a result of the increased momentum it picked up over hundreds of miles. What starts off as a small storm ends up as a killer hurricane.

This is also true of revivals and different moves of God. A move of God is sometimes typified by wind. It is the moving of the winds of the Spirit. They usually start with a small group of people and pick up momentum. The result can be millions swept into the kingdom of God over a period of time.

Another example of momentum is a sports team that wins a few games. Before long this team is on a winning streak. As the team wins, it picks up momentum. One of the hardest things to do is defeat a team that is on a winning streak. Because the team has momentum, it becomes harder to stop the winning streak. The rule in sports is the team that gets momentum is usually the team that wins. *The key is to get and maintain momentum.*

The Lord desires to give *you* momentum. It will carry you into realms of the spirit that you will never enter without it. Satan desires to stop your momentum. He knows that if you get momentum, you will have a greater impact on those around you. Churches that get momentum are churches that will impact their cities. The Body of Christ needs a revelation of how to get momentum, maintain it, and use it to our advantage to fulfill the great commission.

Increasing Your Momentum

And Saul said to David, Thou art not able to go against this Philistine to fight with him: for thou art but a youth, and he a man of war from his youth.

And David said unto Saul, Thy servant kept his father's sheep, and there came a lion, and a bear, and took a lamb out of the flock:

And I went out after him, and smote him, and delivered it out of his mouth: and when he arose against me, I caught him by his beard, and smote him, and slew him.

Thy servant slew both the lion and the bear: and this uncircumcised Philistine shall be as one of them, seeing he has defied the armies of the living God.

David said moreover, The Lord that delivered me out of the paw of the lion, and out of the paw of the bear, he will deliver me out of the hand of this Philistine. And Saul said unto David, Go, and the Lord be with thee.

1 Samuel 17:33-37

One of the keys to getting momentum is to allow your victories to thrust you into greater momentum. David's previous victories gave him the momentum he needed to defeat Goliath. He rehearsed his victories over the lion and the bear *before* he went into battle against the giant. Each victory the Lord gives you increases your momentum. You should always go into battle with momentum from your previous victory.

2

Momentum builds your confidence. It increases your strength and skill for the next battle. True champions understand momentum. They know how to get it and maintain it to achieve victory. True leaders also understand the importance of momentum.

Great generals understand its importance in the field of battle. They know how to capitalize on their opponent's errors and gain momentum in battle. Once they gain momentum, they know how to use it to defeat their foes. Two of Israel's greatest generals were Joshua and David. They understood the place of momentum in warfare. Both used momentum to destroy their enemies.

Great Leaders Understand Momentum

I have pursued mine enemies, and overtaken them: neither did I turn again till they were consumed.

Then did I beat them small as the dust before the wind: I did cast them out as the dirt in the streets.

Psalm 18:37,42

David knew how to get momentum and use it against the enemy. Once he got the upper hand, he pressed the battle and did not turn until he consumed his enemies. He did not stop with a slight victory, he rode his momentum until he *slaughtered* the enemy. David understood the importance of momentum.

Once the Lord gives you momentum, you must use it to your advantage. Don't stop after a slight victory. Continue until the enemy is ROUTED.

Once David had his enemies on the run, he *pursued* and *overtook* them. He consumed them and beat them "as the dust before the wind". He allowed nothing to stop his momentum. He knew his momentum came from the Lord. He knew that once the Lord gave it to him, he had to use it to fulfill His purpose.

There are too many of the Lord's people who stop after a victory. Instead of using that victory as momentum for the next battle, they relax and lose it. The period following a victory is not the time to relax. There are more battles to fight and victories to be won. There are Goliaths to be faced after you defeat your lion and your bear.

Be like David. Pursue, overtake, and consume the enemy! Be persistent and press the battle. Once the Lord gives you the upper hand, have no mercy on Satan and his demons. Use your momentum to your advantage.

Joshua's Momentum

Then spake Joshua to the Lord in the day when the Lord delivered up the Amorites before the children of Israel, and he said in the sight of Israel, Sun, stand thou still upon Gibeon; and thou, Moon, in the valley of Ajalon.

And the sun stood still, and the moon stayed, until the people had avenged themselves upon their enemies. Is not this written in the book of Jasher? So the sun stood still in the midst of heaven, and hasted not to go down about a whole day.

And there was no day like that before it or after it, that the Lord hearkened unto the voice of a man: for the Lord fought for Israel.

Joshua 10:12-14

One of the greatest miracles recorded in the Word of God occurred on the field of battle. Joshua spoke and the Sun and Moon stayed. Joshua received an extra day to defeat his enemies. Joshua understood momentum. Once he saw the enemy's defeat, he would not allow the sun to go down. This miracle gave him the momentum he needed to destroy his enemies. Joshua did not allow darkness to come and stop his momentum. He kept it, *by a miracle,* to destroy the enemy.

Momentum, the Key to Victory

Candidates who get momentum win elections. One issue can give a candidate the momentum needed to win. Armies who get momentum win battles. One strategic advantage can give an army the momentum needed to win.

4

A Russian Winter Can Stop Your Momentum

Adolf Hitler and Nazi Germany had momentum at the beginning of World War II. Through a battle plan called "blitzkrieg," they were able to invade countries through the element of surprise and win quick, easy victories. Germany was winning the war through momentum. However, the allies eventually stopped Hitler's momentum.

A turning point in World War II was the battle of Stalingrad in Russia. Temperatures plunged to -40 degrees Fahrenheit. Troops lacked warm clothing and suffered frostbite. Tanks and weapons broke down. The Russian winter stopped Hitler's troops and over 300,000 were killed or captured. From that point, the momentum began to change and it was a matter of time before Hitler and Germany fell.

Napoleon's armies swept across Europe. Because of his momentum his armies were unstoppable. Ironically, his momentum was also stopped by a Russian winter when he decided to invade Moscow. Of the 600,000 men in Napoleon's forces, over 500,000 were killed, captured or died from illness. Hitler could have learned from Napoleon that a Russian winter can stop an army's momentum.

Miracles Give Us Momentum

Miracles have the power to release momentum. The Lord desires to work miracles through His people to give us the momentum we need to impact our nation for God. Miracles have the power to sweep multitudes into the Kingdom in a short period of time. The ministry of Jesus impacted the entire nation because of miracles.

> **And Jesus went about all Galilee, teaching in their synagogues, and preaching the gospel of the kingdom, and healing all manner of sickness and all manner of disease among the people.**
>
> **And his fame went throughout all Syria: and they brought unto him all sick people that were taken with divers diseases and torments, and those which were pos-**

sessed with devils, and those which were lunatick, and those that had the palsy; and he healed them.

And there followed him great multitudes of people from Galilee and from Decapolis, and from Jerusalem, and from Judaea, and from beyond Jordan.

Matthew 4:23-25

The ministry of Jesus gained tremendous momentum because of the miracles He performed. It was not long before multitudes of people followed Him. Jesus gained such momentum until the religious leaders figured that only His death would stop it. They plotted to kill Jesus in order to stop His momentum.

Then gathered the chief priests and the Pharisees a council, and said, What do we? for this man doeth many miracles.

If we let him thus alone, all men will believe on him: and the Romans shall come and take away both our place and nation.

John 11:47-48

Much people of the Jews therefore knew that he was there: and they came not for Jesus' sake only, but that they might see Lazarus also, whom he had raised from the dead.

But the chief priests consulted that they might put Lazarus also to death;

Because that by reason of him many of the Jews went away, and believed on Jesus.

On the next day much people that were come to the feast, when they heard that Jesus was coming to Jerusalem,

Took branches of palm trees, and went forth to meet him, and cried, Hosanna: BLESSED IS THE KING OF ISRAEL THAT COMETH IN THE NAME OF THE LORD.

The Pharisees therefore said among themselves, Perceive ye how ye prevail nothing? behold, the world is gone after him.

John 12:9-13,19

6

The raising of Lazarus from the dead was the "straw that broke the camel's back". The religious leaders were so upset and worried about the *momentum* of the Lord's ministry that they even consulted to put Lazarus to death. There is no substitute for miracles.

Miracles are a manifestation of God's power in the earth that breaks the power of demonic strongholds and sets people free to receive the truth of the gospel. People will always be attracted to miracles. There is something in all of us that desires to see the supernatural. Some have called healing and miracles "God's dinner bell to salvation".

When the religious leaders were attempting to stop the momentum of the early Church, the prayer of God's people was for the Lord to stretch forth His hand to heal and perform signs and wonders by the name of Jesus (Acts 4:30).

Signs and wonders not only *give* us momentum but they help us *maintain* momentum. A church with miracles is a church that will continue to march triumphantly throughout the land.

One deliverance. One miracle. One healing. One vision. One prophetic word. One relationship is all it takes to start *momentum*. One sermon you hear. One conference you attend. One prophetic word you receive....can break you through and give you the momentum you need to go forth and be a success!

Don't despise the day of small things. Remember, hurricanes start out as small storms that pick up momentum. You may not be doing much now, but take a step at a time and pick up momentum as you go. Once you receive and maintain momentum, it will carry you great distances.

Chapter 2
David's Momentum

Now there was long war between the house of Saul and the house of David: but David WAXED STRONGER AND STRONGER, and the house of Saul waxed weaker and weaker.

2 Samuel 3:1

And David went on, and grew great, and the Lord God of hosts was with him.

2 Samuel 5:10

Those who get momentum will prevail. David eventually gained momentum in his war with the house of Saul. The Rotherham translation says he "went on and on waxing great". The American translation says, "kept on increasing in power".

In the long struggle between David and Saul, it looked at times as if David would lose his life. David even said himself: *"I shall now perish one day by the hand of Saul..."* (1 Samuel 27:1). David found himself fleeing Saul and dwelling in the land of the Philistines, the enemies' camp.

Saul pursued David in the caves and mountains of Israel, and the Lord graciously delivered David from his enemy. After the death of Saul, there was a long war between David and Saul's son, Ishbosheth. Abner, the captain of Ishbosheth's army, fought against Joab, the captain of David's army.

Now David begins to get *momentum*. He gets stronger and stronger, while his enemies get weaker and weaker.

The Scripture states that David went on and grew "great". His momentum not only carried him to the throne to be king over Israel, but it carried him to victory over Israel's enemies.

> **And David did so, as the Lord had commanded him; and smote the Philistines from Geba until thou come to Gazer.**
>
> **2 Samuel 5:25**

> **And after this it came to pass, that David smote the Philistines, and subdued them: and David took Methegammah out of the hand of the Philistines.**
>
> **And he smote Moab, and measured them with a line, casting them down to the ground;...**
>
> **David smote also Hadadezer, the son of Rehob, king of Zobah,...**
>
> **..., David slew of the Syrians two and twenty thousand men.**
>
> **..., and all they of Edom became David's servants....**
>
> **2 Samuel 8:1-3,5,14**

David was, what we call today, "on a roll". He harnessed his momentum and maintained it to defeat his enemies within Israel and without. Each victory gave him increased momentum for his next challenge.

We go from strength to strength, faith to faith, and glory to glory.

Absalom's Momentum

Not only can momentum work for you, but it can work against you. Even wickedness, if not stopped, will gain momentum. David's momentum of victories came to an end because of his sin of adultery with Bathsheba, and murder of Uriah, her husband. This opened the door for the enemy to use his son, Absalom, against him. Absalom gained momentum against his father. His conspiracy grew stronger and stronger.

And the conspiracy was strong; for the people *increased continually* with Absalom.

2 Samuel 15:12

This shows us the power of *momentum*. Once anything gains momentum, whether good or evil, it is hard to stop. Because David was not able to "nip it in the bud", the conspiracy of Absalom grew stronger and gained momentum.

And there came a messenger to David, saying, The hearts of the men of Israel are after Absalom.

And David said unto all his servants that were with him at Jerusalem, Arise, and let us flee; for we shall not else escape from Absalom: make speed to depart, lest he overtake us suddenly,...

2 Samuel 15:13,14

David had to flee for his life. The momentum for evil was so strong that he did not have the strength to stop it. Only David's prayers and God's intervention were strong enough to stop Absalom's momentum.

David gave his enemies momentum against him through his foolishness. Sin not only can stop your momentum, but it can also give the enemy momentum *against* you. This is why it is imperative that we maintain our momentum by avoiding sin and foolishness. Give no place to the devil (Ephesians 5).

Keep your momentum over the enemy. Never allow him to get momentum over you. One sinful act can destroy your momentum. One foolish act can destroy your momentum. One costly mistake can stop your momentum.

One Achan stopped Israel's momentum. One sin stopped David's momentum.

And it came to pass, after the year was expired, at the time when kings go forth to battle, that David sent Joab,..... But David tarried still at Jerusalem.

2 Samuel 11:1

This was the beginning of David's troubles. Instead of going forth to battle as the leader of God's people, he stayed at Jerusalem and sent Joab to battle. David had just slew the Syrians destroying seven hundred chariots and forty thousand horsemen in a previous battle (2 Samuel 10:18). This gives us an important truth: *Don't stop after a victory. Keep your momentum!* Remember, a victory gives you momentum for the next battle.

Instead of going forth into battle, David remained in Jerusalem and fell into adultery with Bathsheba (2 Samuel 11:2-5). David relaxed and fell into sin. He lost his momentum, and his string of victories came to an end. This opened the way for the enemy to bring much sadness and grief into his life. David almost lost his kingdom as a result. This hidden sin stopped his momentum. Although he tried to hide it and cover it up, it caused him eventual shame and dishonor.

The Lord of Bursts

And David came to Baalperazim, and David smote them there, and said, The Lord hath broken forth upon mine enemies before me, as a breach of waters....

2 Samuel 5:20

David describes his momentum from the Lord as a breach of waters. The Rotherham translation says, "like a breaking forth of waters". The Moffat translation says, "like waters bursting a dam". He called the name of the place "Baal-perazim", which means *lord of bursts.*

To *burst* means to force open (as a door) by strong or vigorous action. It means to break open, apart, or into pieces — usually from *impact* or from pressure within. Remember, the key to impact is momentum. The greater the momentum, the greater the impact. The Lord wants to give you so much momentum that you literally burst forth upon your enemies.

When a dam breaks, the momentum from the rushing waters will destroy everything in its path. Your momentum can be like a mighty rushing river, destroying and overtaking any opposition from the devil in your path.

Chapter 3
Dunamis

And, behold, I send the promise of my Father upon you: but tarry ye in the city of Jerusalem, until ye be endued with power from on high.

Luke 24:49

The Church started with momentum. The day of Pentecost was a day of momentum for the Church. *Dunamis* is the Greek word for *power*. Dunamis gives the Church *momentum*.

Momentum is the result of power. The more powerful a thing becomes, the more momentum it carries, and the more momentum a thing receives the more power it has. Momentum and impact are related to THRUST. To *thrust* means to push or drive with force. The force needed to thrust the Church forward was "dunamis", the power of the Holy Ghost.

The day of Pentecost gave the Church the momentum it needed to invade the world with the gospel. From Jerusalem, the Church moved forward with and maintained its momentum to impact the world with the message of Salvation.

...and the same day there were added unto them about three thousand souls.

Acts 2:41

Howbeit many of them which heard the word believed; and the number of the men was about five thousand.

Acts 4:4

13

And believers were the more added to the Lord, multitudes both men and women.

Acts 5:14

There came also a multitude out of the cities round about unto Jerusalem, bringing sick folks, and them which were vexed with unclean spirits: and they were healed every one.

Then the high priest rose up, and all they that were with him, (which is the sect of the Sadducees,) and were filled with indignation,

Acts 5:16-17

Persecution is an attempt by the enemy to stop momentum. The first opposition the early Church encountered was from the established *religious system* of their day. Every revival and move of God is fought by *religion*. Those who want to maintain the status quo don't like change.

We must have enough momentum to break through persecution. Never allow persecution for righteousness' sake to stop your momentum. Never allow what people say or do to stop your momentum, if you are in the will of God. Recognize persecution as an attempt by Satan to stop your momentum. You cannot react to it in the flesh, but you must respond to it in the Spirit.

...and when they had called the apostles and beaten them, they commanded that they should not speak in the name of Jesus, and let them go.

And they departed from the presence of the council, rejoicing that they were counted worthy to suffer shame for his name.

Acts 5:40-41

The apostles did not allow the persecution to stop their momentum. They responded to a physical beating by REJOICING. *"And daily in the temple, and in every house, they ceased not to teach and preach Jesus Christ"* (Acts 5:42). They did not *cease* to teach and preach. Once you gain momentum in any endeavor, don't cease! Learning how to maintain your momentum in the face of *opposition* is a key to your success.

14

The Result of Momentum

Even after threats and beatings from the religious leaders, the apostles kept their momentum.

And the word of God increased; and the number of disciples multiplied in Jerusalem greatly; and a great company of the priests were obedient to the faith.

Acts 6:7

Increase and multiplication are the result of momentum. Even the strongest opponent of the Church, Saul, was changed and became the apostle Paul. This shows us the power of momentum. *The enemy will not be able to stop a church with momentum.* When the Lord's people gain momentum, it will cause our enemies to either be destroyed or *converted.*

After the conversion of Saul, the Church had rest throughout all Judea and Galilee, and Samaria, and *"were multiplied"* (Acts 9:31). When a move of God gains momentum, it will sweep everything in its path. People will either be swept into it or be destroyed by it.

Herod

Now about that time Herod the king stretched forth his hands to vex certain of the church.

And he killed James the brother of John with the sword.

And because he saw it pleased the Jews, he proceeded further to take Peter also....

Acts 12:1-3

One of the ways the enemy stops the momentum of a move of God is to attack its leaders. Every move of God has leaders. Herod killed James and was planning to kill Peter. The church prayed day and night for Peter's release. Because of angelic intervention, Peter was set free from prison. Not only did an angel deliver Peter but an angel smote Herod, and he was eaten of worms (Acts 12:23). If the enemy can discourage or eliminate a leader, he is often successful in stopping the momentum of a *Move.*

But the word of God grew and multiplied.

Acts 12:24

The Phillips translation says, "But the word of the Lord continued to gain ground and increase its influence." Herod was destroyed, and the Church maintained its momentum. Leaders need prayer. They need intercessors to stand with them in order to keep their momentum. Intercession and prayer help us maintain momentum in the face of opposition.

Boldness Helps Us Maintain Momentum

And now, Lord, behold their threatenings: and grant unto thy servants, that with all boldness they may speak thy word.

By stretching forth thine hand to heal; and that signs and wonders may be done by the name of thy holy child Jesus.

Acts 4:29-30

The threatenings of the religious leaders were intended to stop the momentum of the early Church. They prayed for *boldness* that would result from signs and wonders. Fear will stop your momentum. The fear of man brings a snare. Fear will paralyze you. It is a spirit from hell, sent to stop you. Boldness will rise up in your spirit to overcome opposition. Anyone who gains momentum will encounter resistance.

The enemy will not just sit back and watch you go forth and establish the kingdom of God without resistance. He will attempt to stop you through fear. Boldness helps us maintain momentum. Instead of drawing back, the apostles *"were all filled with the Holy Ghost, and they spake the word of God with boldness"* (Acts 4:31).

Through boldness they overcame the opposition of the enemy. Many believers give up the moment they encounter *resistance.* They lose their momentum and stop doing what the Lord has commanded them to do. Pray for boldness. Rise up in courage and continue in spite of intimidation.

And when they had gone through the isle unto Paphos, they found a certain sorcerer, a false prophet, a Jew, whose name was Barjesus:

Acts 13:6

If the enemy cannot stop you through fear and intimidation, he will attempt to stop you through *deception*. Paul and Barnabus encountered a sorcerer named Barjesus on their first missionary journey. He withstood them (Acts 13:8). Paul called judgment down upon him, and he was smitten blind.

Paul called him, *"O full of all subtilty and all mischief"*. The Twentieth Century New Testament says: "You incarnation of deceit and fraud." The Williams translation says: "You expert in every form of deception and sleight-of-hand."

Satan will use *men* to stop your momentum. One bad relationship can stop your momentum. One good relationship can give you momentum.

When Israel came out of Egypt they had momentum. When Balak (the king of Moab) saw Israel, he called for Balaam to come and curse them. He tried to use witchcraft to stop their progress.

Chapter 4
Thieves of Momentum

O foolish Galatians, who hath bewitched you, that ye should not obey the truth,...

Galatians 3:1

Ye did run well; who did hinder you that ye should not obey the truth?

Galatians 5:7

The Knox translation says: "Senseless Galatians, who is it that has cast a spell on you."

Coming under the control of another is *witchcraft*, which puts you under a spell. The Goodspeed translation of Galatians 5:7 says: "You were making such progress."

Beware of wrong relationships. Controllers and manipulators will stop your momentum. The Galatians had lost their momentum by allowing themselves to come under the control of legalistic teachers. Beware of Legalism. *It will stop your spiritual momentum.*

Stand fast in liberty. Maintain your liberty and freedom in the Spirit. Stay free in the Spirit. Follow the cloud of God. Some people are stuck in previous moves of God. They stopped to build a monument. They refused to move on with God into the next move. Every move of God is designed to give you momentum for the next move. Momentum will carry you from one move to the next. Let nothing stop you from obeying God.

Religious control will stop your momentum. Too many believers allow religious control to stop them. Control spirits

19

are of the devil. Relationships based on fear, control and intimidation are of the devil. Relationships from God will help you get and maintain your momentum. Relationships from the devil will cause you to stop and lose your momentum.

Sin Stops Momentum

So there went up thither of the people about three thousand men: and they fled before the men of Ai.

And the men of Ai smote of them about thirty and six men: for they chased them from before the gate even unto Shebarim, and smote them in the going down: wherefore the hearts of the people melted, and became as water.

Joshua 7:4-5

Ai was the second battle Israel fought after they entered Canaan. The first battle was Jericho. They destroyed Jericho and seemed to have the momentum they needed to defeat Ai. Even though Ai seemed to be an easy victory in the natural, they were turned back in defeat. Achan had brought a curse upon Israel by partaking of the accursed thing.

As a result, Israel could not stand before their enemies. Because of one man's trespass Israel lost their momentum. They were brought to a virtual standstill. Joshua had to pray and receive revelation as to why Israel fell before Ai.

Joshua 7:1 calls the act a "trespass". The word *trespass* is the Hebrew word *maal* meaning sin falsehood, transgression. It also means treachery, to act covertly or treacherously, to cover up. This is exactly what Achan did. He tried to cover up his sin by hiding the garment and the silver he had coveted.

This gives us a clue as to what stops momentum. Not only does sin stop our momentum, but *hidden* sins. The hidden sin of Achan stopped the momentum and forward progress of Joshua and the armies of Israel.

Jericho was a great victory. After Jericho fell, every nation in Canaan heard of its defeat. This great victory gave Israel the momentum it needed to go forth and possess Canaan. Remember, every victory gives you momentum for the next battle. Israel should have had no problem with Ai. It was a small city compared to Jericho. The Israelites were so sure of victory until they did not send their entire army against it. But the defeat by Ai came as a result of a *hidden sin*.

Hidden sins will destroy your momentum. Anything that can stop your momentum, needs to be eliminated from your life. Any relationship, habit, or act that leads you into sin, must be eliminated from your life if you are to maintain your *spiritual momentum*.

Ask yourself this question: *What is the one thing that always stops my momentum?* Is it a particular habit that you cannot seem to break? Is it a relationship that you cannot seem to shake? Is it anger, lust, fear, discouragement, depression, hurt, bitterness, unforgiveness? Whatever it is that stops your momentum, you must isolate it and eliminate it from your life. There is no hidden sin worth stopping your momentum.

Procrastination is a thief of momentum. Jesus knew at an early age that He must be about his Father's business. Some people always dream about tomorrow without ever doing anything today. What you do today will determine whether you will have momentum tomorrow. Momentum is a result of action.

Procrastinators are full of excuses. You must eliminate every excuse that stops you from doing what you have been called to do. Moses' excuse was his speech. Jeremiah's was his youth. There is no excuse worth stopping your momentum. God's grace is sufficient. Winners don't allow excuses to stop them from winning.

Passivity and *slothfulness* are two more thieves of momentum. Some people are too passive and lazy to gain momentum. Momentum comes to *doers* of the Word.

A double minded man is unstable in all his ways.

James 1:8

Double mindedness will rob you of momentum. Some people never get momentum because they never decide to do anything. They are too indecisive. They can never make up their minds as to which direction they should go. The Goodspeed translation says, "an irresolute person like him, who is uncertain about everything he does". The Weymouth translation says, "being a man of two minds, undecided in every step he takes".

Momentum will carry you to your destination, but you must set your course. You must take the first step. Momentum always begins with a first step, a decision. Don't allow doublemindedness to keep you from taking the first step. Decide to do something. Be a person of action. Jesus knew his Father's will and moved in that direction. You may start off slow but as you gain momentum, you will begin to see results. A thousand mile journey begins with one small step.

Regaining Your Momentum

But mine enemies are lively, and they are strong: and they that hate me wrongfully are multiplied.

Psalm 38:19

When David sinned, he lost his momentum and gave his enemies an advantage. David's enemies had momentum against him. Either *you* have momentum or your enemy has momentum. David's sin caused him to lose his momentum. Absalom gained momentum and used it to attempt to take the kingdom. Throughout the Psalms, David prayed and repented. This gives us an important *key* to regaining our momentum — Repentance.

O spare me, that I may recover strength, before I go hence, and be no more.

Psalm 39:13

When we have lost our momentum, and the enemy has gained momentum, we need the mercy of the Lord. Only the Lord can stop the enemy's momentum.

...let them be driven backward and put to shame that with me evil.

Psalm 40:14

Prayer and fasting will help you regain your momentum. Prayer and fasting will lift up a standard against the enemy. Fasting turns back the armies of the enemy (Joel 2:20).

I humbled my soul with fasting,...

Psalm 35:13

My knees are weak through fasting; and my flesh faileth of fatness.

Psalm 109:24

When David's enemies prevailed, he used that key of fasting to stop the enemies' momentum. Through prayer and fasting, he regained the momentum he lost. The battle was turned against his enemies in his favor. Prayer and fasting causes the enemy to be *turned back.* You must have the knowledge to take away the enemy's momentum and regain yours. Even so, it is better to maintain your momentum and never lose it.

On the other hand, if you have lost your momentum, don't give up! There is a way to regain it through *repentance, prayer and fasting.* We must remember that our God is the Father of mercies (2 Corinthians 1:3). We can come boldly to the throne of grace and obtain mercy, and find grace, to help in the time of need (Hebrews 4:16).

The Lord will hear your prayer, release His mercy, restore you, and cause you to regain your momentum. If you have lost your momentum, spend some time in fasting and prayer. You will begin to see your spiritual and physical life invigorated.

Although David fell, he knew the Lord was merciful, and his repentance, prayer and fasting caused him to regain his momentum, and to be restored in God's kingdom.

To order books and tapes by
John Eckhardt,
please write or call:

Crusaders Ministries
6150 W. North Avenue
Chicago, IL 60639
(312) 637-2121